May the Angels Carry You

דעת DA'AT INSTITUTE

DEATH AWARENESS, ADVOCACY *and* TRAINING

Jewish Life, Death, and Transition Series

Other Titles from the Series

The Grief Journey and the Afterlife:
Jewish Pastoral Care for the Bereavement

Living and Dying in Ancient Times:
Death, Burial, and Mourning in Biblical Tradition

May the Angels Carry You

Jewish Prayers and Meditations for the Deathbed

Simcha Paull Raphael

Albion
Andalus
Boulder, Colorado
2016

*"The old shall be renewed,
and the new shall be made holy."*
— Rabbi Avraham Yitzhak Kook

Albion-Andalus, Inc.
P. O. Box 19852
Boulder, CO 80308
www.albionandalus.com

Design and layout by Albion-Andalus Books
Cover design by Daryl McCool, D.A.M. Cool Graphics
Cover image by Geela Rayzel Raphael

ISBN-13: 978-0692765609 (Albion-Andalus Books)
ISBN-10: 0692765603

In memory of colleagues and friends
who left this world in the prime years of life

Rabbi Ron Aigen, z"l
Rabbi Devora Bartnoff, z"l
Rabbi Aryeh Hirschfield, z"l
Lisa Kapin, z"l
Cantor Chaim Rothstein, z"l
Rabbi David Wolfe-Blank, z"l

May the spirit of their teachings and
the songs they sang be remembered
as a source of love, wisdom and blessings!

CONTENTS

Preface   xi
Foreword by Rabbi Nadya Gross   xix

Introduction   1
   What Does It Mean to Pray for
   Someone Who Is Dying?

Shema Yisrael   17
   The Eternal Our God is One

V'ahavta   19
   And You Shall Love *Adonai* Your God

The Priestly Blessing   23

Mi Shebeirach   25
   A Prayer for Healing

B'Shem HaShem   27
   Angel Song

Gesher Tzar Me'od   29
   A Very Narrow Bridge

Psalm 121   31
   A Song of Ascents

Vidui   33
  A Prayer of Transition
  Recited by One Who is Dying

Vidui   37
  A Prayer of Transition
  Recited On Behalf of One Who is Dying

A *Techinah* for the Deathbed   41

Exercise   45
  Writing One's Personal *Vidui*

May the Angels Carry You   49
  A *Vidui* Song

Vidui: Meditations of Transition   51
  1. Purification/Opening to the World Beyond
  2. Invoking the Angels
  3. Leaving Go of the Physical Body

Prayer for When Life Support   61
Is Being Removed

Ana B'Koach   65
  Source of Mercy

Life Review, Legacy and Words   67
of Comfort

Pondering the Mysteries of
Life and Death   69

Afterlife Journey of the Soul   73
in Kabbalah

Deathbed Stories of the   85
Hasidic Masters

Psalms of Healing   89

Crossing the Bar   91

For Further Reading   93
Notes and References   95
May the Angels Carry You   99
Album information
About the DA'AT Institute   101

PREFACE

A STORY IS TOLD of an elderly Jewish woman whose death was imminent. In a desire to be helpful, her daughter planned to read her mother selections from the *Tibetan Book of the Dead*, a sixteenth century deathbed manual created by Tibetan Buddhist monks. However, Stephen Levine, a spiritual teacher known for his innovative deathbed work, cautioned her against doing so. The arcane symbolism of the *Tibetan Book of the Dead*, he explained, would only frighten and confuse the elderly woman. Instead, he encouraged the daughter to read her dying mother Yiddish love songs.[1]

I have always found this story to be emblematic of the cultural deficit of Jewish resources for end-of-life care. While Yiddish love songs have an emotional and sentimental quality for an elderly Jewish "Bubby," are there not philosophical teachings and liturgical traditions of Judaism to offer comfort and spiritual nourishment when people are dying? Traditions of ancient deathbed manuals are found all across the globe—the *Tibetan Book of the Dead*, the *Egyptian Book of the Dead*, the Christian *Ars Moriendi*, as well as lesser-known Mesoamerican Toltec, Aztec and Mayan books of the dead—all of which offer liturgies for dying and teachings on the postmortem journey of the soul.[2] And Judaism? Are Yiddish love songs the only prescribed resource for meeting the needs of the dying and their families? Something seems amiss here.

The reality is that something *is* amiss. With modernity, secularization and assimilation over the past two centuries, we lost touch with many of the historical resources Judaism traditionally provided for dealing with dying and the deathbed. Most contemporary Jews (and non-Jews) are more familiar with the *Tibetan Book of the Dead* than with texts such as *Ma'avor Yabok* (17th-century Italy) and *Sefer HaHayim* (18th-century Holland),[3] to name but two classical Jewish texts with liturgies and prayers for attending to the needs of the sick, dying and dead.

In circulation for centuries, these texts— as well as at least a dozen others[4]—were widely distributed in the Jewish communities of Eastern, Central and Southern Europe.[5] However, today they are largely unknown in North American Jewish life. Even more: many contemporary Jews are not even aware that the deathbed confession—the *vidui*, a Jewish prayer specifically for end-of-life transition—was once normative and ubiquitous to Jewish community life. With the migrational movement from Eastern and Central Europe to North America, and the shift away from knowledge of Yiddish and Hebrew, the deathbed *vidui* seemed to disappear, relegated in the past century to a small chapter in the "Rabbi's manual,"[6] and, as a result, inaccessible to most Jews.

It is not that Jewish deathbed resources do not exist; the simple fact of the matter is that they are mostly unknown to many Jews (and non-Jews with Jewish family members) who need such resources when dealing with end-of-life transitions.

In my work as a hospice chaplain, I often encountered families totally unfamiliar with Jewish deathbed traditions. They knew one could recite a Psalm, or a healing prayer on behalf of a family member who was dying, and usually requested a rabbi to do it for them. But overall, facing the imminent death of a loved one, most Jewish families I met in hospice and pastoral counseling settings were ritually unequipped to deal with death, all too often feeling disempowered and spiritually overwhelmed in the liminal moments at the end of life.

It is not as if they could easily go to a bookstore and find a book of Jewish prayers for the deathbed.

There are books on Jewish mourning rituals and practices, but contemporary Jewish prayer manuals for the deathbed, generally speaking, do not exist now as they did two hundred years ago.[7] So given that Jewish deathbed practices are hardly known today, it makes sense that in a time of need a Jewish woman whose mother was dying might turn to the *Tibetan Book of the Dead*, or similar non-Jewish resources.

Yet, in its wisdom, Judaism teaches: "To everything there is a season; a time to be born, a time to die." These well-known words from the Book of Ecclesiastes affirm the essential Jewish teaching that death and human mortality are inherently part of life. Judaism honors the sacredness of life, but also realistically acknowledges that human beings encounter illness, dying, and death. When this happens, we know people need the kind of medical support provided by doctors, nurses, hospitals, and hospices; and emotional and spiritual support offered by mental health professionals, chaplains and pastoral care-givers. But along with medical care and psycho-spiritual comfort, at the bedside of one who is dying, individuals and families also yearn for practical tools and functional resources to facilitate the tender moments of death's gentle arrival, and the ebbing of consciousness as it departs from the body.

At such times holding a dying person's hand, sitting in silence, or listening to music all can be very helpful. In addition, Jewish prayers, song, chant, meditations, and reflective readings have the ability to impart efficacious ritual meaning and a comforting spiritual balm for heart, mind and soul. It is exactly these kinds of resources that this book offers—a simple and functional end-of-life tool kit for the dying and their families.

May the Angels Carry You provides an assortment of traditional and contemporary Jewish prayers—all in English, some in Hebrew and in transliteration—as well as meditations and sacred readings. This book is designed to be a functional 21st-century deathbed manual for those who are on an end-of-life journey, and for those who accompany them.

Having spent time sitting in silence with the dying, singing prayers, chanting Psalms, reciting the deathbed confession and talking with spouses, siblings, children, and grandchildren of the dying about death and the world beyond, I sensed the need for a hands-on resource people could use at the bedside. Designed to provide emotional comfort and spiritual wisdom, *May the Angels Carry You* is a cookbook more than a technological "how-to" manual, not to be read cover to cover, but rather to be used as needed for different moments of companioning the dying and seeking personal meaning and solace in the face of life's finitude. It is my hope that those chanting the prayers and reading the reflections found within this book will find consolation and connection with the divine as they "walk through the valley of the shadow of death."

This is the third book in the *Jewish Life, Death and Transition* series, published by Albion-Andalus Books, in collaboration with the DA'AT Institute for Death Awareness, Advocacy and Training. I thank Netanel Miles-Yépez of Albion-Andalus Books for his vision to create this series, and his editorial wisdom and patience in bringing this book to publication.

Additionally, my sincere thanks to Rabbi Tsurah August, of the Jewish Hospice Network, of Jewish Family and Children's Service in Philadelphia, Pennsylvania, from whom I learned a great deal about being a comforting presence for the dying and their families; to my friend and colleague Rabbi Nadya Gross, for authoring the Foreword and offering me both professional support and genuine friendship in the creation of this book; to David Zinner of Kavod v'Nichum, as well Rabbinic Pastor De Herman, Rabbi Chaya Gusfield, and Amy Grossblatt Pessah for thoughtful editorial feedback on the manuscript of this book. Furthermore, I wish to express my profound appreciation for the technical artistry of my friend, Baruch Sienna of Aleph Technology who prepared the Hebrew texts that embellish the pages of *May the Angels Carry You*.

I am also ever-grateful for the influence and mentorship of my teacher, Rabbi Zalman Schachter-Shalomi, of Blessed Memory, who inspired, motivated and guided my work in exploring Jewish views of death and the afterlife. Even though my teacher Reb Zalman has passed over to the world beyond, the gift of his teaching and his legacy continues to grow. I can imagine the smile on his face upon seeing this book in his hand.

To my children, Yigdal and Hallel, I offer thanks for putting up with my death humor, and for teaching me what is truly important in life.

Finally, to my wife Rabbi Geela Rayzel Raphael, I offer heart-felt thanks and appreciation for being a constant companion on the spiritual, professional and personal journey of my life over the past three decades. I know you are there in support of my work in the world. I am also delighted and appreciative to be able to use your artwork for the cover of this book, and to have your music—an album also titled *May the Angels Carry You*—as a companion to this volume! Thank you!

I am grateful for the opportunity to share the fruits of my own learning with others, and with devotion, I acknowledge the Source of Life, the Holy One of Blessing who has given us life and vitality, sustained us and brought us to this moment.

— SIMCHA PAULL RAPHAEL, PH.D.,
Melrose Park, PA
July 1, 2016
The occasion of my 65th birthday

Foreword

MY FATHER WAS 49 years old when he died of cancer. A quintessential salesman, he loved making friends wherever he went, and people responded in kind to his open-hearted nature. So when word got out about his battle with this dreaded disease, one would have expected to have to fend off a legion of visitors. While there were many calls and cards, expressing love, dismay and support, few came to sit by his bedside. It was baffling.

The synagogue where my father had been an active member, volunteer, and beloved Hebrew teacher for almost fifteen years had hired a newly-minted young rabbi right around the time we learned of his diagnosis. When the rabbi finally made his obligatory hospital visit, just weeks before my father's death, I was shocked at his obvious discomfort. It was clear to me that he simply did not know how to be there. He offered no words of comfort or prayer to my father, nor to any of us, his family members, who were present in the room.

In my future life as a rabbi, I felt a deep, visceral

call to serve the dying and their loved ones, and experienced variations of my father's story time and again. I was facilitating a spiritual support group for people with life-limiting illness, and heard how their friends seemed to disappear. The pain of abandonment at such a critical time in their lives was acute, and it triggered my own memories of confusion and disappointment in my father's friends.

I became a 'field researcher.' I reached out to the friends of my group members, hoping to cajole or inspire them to rekindle their relationships, wanting them to know that their friendship was even more important now than ever before. I learned something that shouldn't have surprised me quite as much as it did. People stay away because they simply don't know how to sit in the presence of illness, suffering, and loss. They don't know what to say or how to behave. So they make every excuse imaginable today— promising themselves they'll find time to visit tomorrow.

Of course, I should have remembered the packed room at my father's funeral, and the countless expressions of regret: "I should have visited" . . . "I never imagined he'd go so soon."

It is a core Jewish value to visit the sick, and Judaism teaches that a dying person is never to be left alone. Our story chests are a treasure trove of deathbed images, the dying surrounded by the prayers and loving wishes of those bringing them comfort. What has become of these traditions?

There was a time when birth and death were natural occurrences in the circle of life. Three generations lived together in the family home. Babies were born in the same bed where grandparents died. Both one's entry into life and the departure were accompanied by family members; sometimes with the aid, in the best of circumstances, of a healer or spiritual adept—a midwife, a *rebbe* or a shaman.

With the advent of modern medicine, these two experiences were moved out of the home and into hospitals. What was once a normal process taking place in one room while children played in another and dinner cooked on the stove, now became something distant, mysterious and frightening—something to be avoided. North America can be labeled as a death-denying society. We have lost our capacity to sit in the presence of illness and death because it is very easy to spend our lives never having to confront it.

My generation has sought to re-normalize the birth process; home births and the practice of midwifery were reinstated as a respected choice. Courses in natural and family-centered childbirth are now part of the options that an expectant parent may choose. In *May the Angels Carry You: Jewish Prayers and Meditations for the Deathbed*, Simcha Paull Raphael is offering this same generation the guidance and support necessary to accompany the dying with skill and confidence. This book contains the tools for those who might otherwise stay away because they don't know what to say. He offers a range of options, from traditional prayers to questions one might ask to facilitate the very kinds of conversations we've learned that those facing death long to engage in.

In his concise review of the efficacy of prayer, one finds the inspiration to overcome what may be a natural resistance to something unfamiliar, and the support needed to recite both the ancient and more contemporary words that have been offered at many bedsides. Those who avail themselves of this guidance will surely be saved the feelings of shame and remorse that I heard at my father's funeral, and so many others since that time.

This book is also a wonderful companion in the hands of the one who is dying. She may take comfort in reading the prayers herself; he may find, in the meditations offered, images that help him begin to make sense of what awaits him after this life ends. Ultimately, these experiences may help them begin to express the thoughts and wishes they need to share with those they are leaving behind.

In its simple and direct approach, Simcha Paull Raphael's beautiful prayer book normalizes death and offers us a path to renew our sacred traditions surrounding the end of life. Jewish law makes it clear that a dying person is considered the same as a living person in every respect. Taking this to heart, one understands that we do not stop cultivating our relationships with those who are dying. With the aid and encouragement of the resources in this book, one can engage intimately with the dying person, capturing her stories and helping to communicate the essence of her life to those who will carry her in their hearts.

In the book, *Tuesdays with Morrie*, the one-time Brandeis University professor dying of ALS tells us: "Death ends a life, not a relationship." May we all be blessed to experience the power of the relationship that remains with us when we have had the opportunity to truly pray for and provide friendship and support to one who is facing the ultimate life transition.

— RABBI NADYA GROSS, Boulder, CO
Director, *Hashpa'ah*: Aleph Training Program for Jewish Spiritual Directors

INTRODUCTION
WHAT DOES IT MEAN TO PRAY FOR SOMEONE WHO IS DYING?

THIS PRAYER BOOK is designed to be a practical resource for people approaching the end of life, and for family members and professional care-givers who companion them on the journey. It is, as the title suggests, a spiritual resource of Jewish prayers and meditations for the deathbed.

But what does it mean to offer prayers on behalf of one who is dying? When reciting Psalms or singing prayers at the bedside of a person whose life force is waning because of a serious illness, or one who may already have been given a terminal diagnosis, how do we understand our goals and imagined outcome? As citizens of the 21st-century who recognize the complexity of medical science, can we assume our prayers will bring someone back from death's door? When feeling powerless in the face of devastating diseases such as cancer, stroke, Parkinson's, Alzheimer's and other forms of dementia, heart disease, etc., do we really believe our prayers will make a difference? What is the function of prayer?

I recall times when serving as a pastoral chaplain in hospice and chronic care settings, it was common for family members to ask "Rabbi, will you say a prayer or a blessing?" While it was easy enough to find the words of a Psalm or a healing prayer to offer on behalf of someone who was sick, speaking with family members about prayer, differences between healing of the body and healing of the soul, and having conversations about God, if people were open to such dialogue, was often even more poignant than the prayers themselves. Today, in addition to words and melodies of prayer, people often need a framework and context to see the deeper processes involved in the act of praying, especially at the deathbed.

In offering these reflections on the function and efficacy of deathbed prayer, my intention is to help make the words and prayers in this book more meaningful to you and those around you. While I recognize that there are no final answers to the ultimate mystery and enigma of human mortality, I hope my thoughts on this complex subject will invite you to reflect on what it means to provide prayer, spiritual support and companionship to loved ones who are "on the runway" preparing for a departure from this world.

Prayer As Dipping Into the
Well of God's Blessings

In exploring the meaning and function of deathbed prayer, it is important to know that the Hebrew word for blessing, *brachah* (plural *berachot),* is derived from the root word *berech*—which also means "knee." The formula that often begins traditional Jewish blessings is *Baruch Atta Adonai*—"Blessed are you God." Interpretatively we can translate this to mean "I bend my knees before you, O God!" The central notion here is that prayer itself is a bending or surrender to divine power or God's potency. Thus, in dealing with sickness and death we surrender our sense of being in control in asking God to be an agent of the healing that we cannot do ourselves.

Taking this traditional point of view one step further: another understanding of the word *brachah*, blessing, is connected to the Hebrew word *bereichah*—a "pool" or a "channel of water flowing down."[8] Thus praying for another person can be seen as dipping into the pool of divine blessing, to bring forth protection or healing to the person for whom we are praying.

In traditional religious language, the notion here is that God's grace and blessings are always available for each person to draw down into their own life, whether we are praying for healing of the body or healing of the soul.

While this is the starting point-of-view for thinking about the function of prayer on the deathbed, the inter-weaving of traditional and contemporary ideas about prayer are much more complicated and diverse.

Prayers for Healing of Body

The traditional Jewish prayer for healing—the *Mi Shebeirach* petitions:

> May the One who blessed our ancestors,
> Abraham, Isaac, and Jacob,
> Sarah, Rebecca, Rachel, and Leah
> bless and heal the one who is ill . . .

Even more, we call upon God as the Merciful One and ask for "a complete healing from the heavenly realm, a healing of body and a healing of soul." So if someone sick and frail is lying in a bed before us, do we really believe our prayers to God can heal them? Oddly enough, modernity and secular rationalism notwithstanding, the answer is a resounding "yes!" In the face of illness of a loved one, we hope against hope, and

4

we pray for their healing. That is certainly one of our conscious or unconscious expectations of prayers for the sick.

As it turns out, our expectations are not completely unfounded.

In recent years there have been somewhat unorthodox, scientific studies demonstrating the potency of healing prayers. American physician and researcher Dr. Larry Dossey has investigated the impact of the human mind and spirituality on physical healing. In his book, *Healing Words: The Power of Prayer and the Practice of Medicine,* Dossey cites research indicating that intercessory prayers offered on behalf of another person can be efficacious in the healing process. For example, in a famous double-blind study at San Francisco General Hospital in 1988, 192 randomly-chosen cardiac patients were prayed for by home prayer groups which were simply given the patients' names. A second group of patients of a similar size did not have any prayer directed their way.

Follow-up study over ten months demonstrated that the prayed-for patients had significantly less deaths, and no one in that group ended up having to use a mechanical respirator. In the second group, however, there were more deaths, and twelve patients required use of a ventilator.

In a similar vein, in a second study with non-human organic matter, twenty specimens of identical bacteria were divided into two groups. The group that had people praying for the speedy growth of the bacteria in the test tube, grew at a more rapid rate. The implications of Dossey's research, based on scores of similar studies, suggest that a loving, caring mental attitude towards another living organism, human or not, has a beneficent healing effect.[9]

Cutting edge scientific research suggests that it is within the realm of human expectations that our prayers can be effective agents of healing. Today, it is very common for families to put out requests for prayers for loved ones undergoing treatment for illness, and particular websites, such as Caring Bridge, have become popular outreach tools that families can use to both communicate news on the medical journey of a family member, and to ask others to offer prayers for healing. While we cannot always guarantee that our prayers will be effective for healing, we do hold out hope that our prayers are "heard" in the highest realms. In this sense, one function of reciting some of the prayers in this book is so that there can be, as the *Mi Shebeirach* says, "a healing of body, a healing of soul."

Prayers for Healing of Soul

A question to ask here is when is it time to recognize that our prayers might not work to save someone's life. Not all prayers for "healing of body" are effective, and often in spite of prayers offered on behalf of someone ill, people still die. Thousands and thousands of individuals all across the planet can say a *Mi Shebeirach* healing prayer for someone with cancer, with no obvious results for physical recovery.

Sometimes people hold a simplistic theology that imagines an all-powerful God who is supposed to answer all of our prayers, all of the time, in all circumstances. And it is certainly not uncommon for a person to think, 'If God has not answered my prayers for healing a loved one, then I can no longer believe in that God.'

But just because prayer *can* be efficacious, it does not mean all prayer for physical healing *is* efficacious. In fact, talmudic tradition even suggests that sometimes prayer for someone who is dying is contraindicated.

A story is told of the death of the sage Yehuda HaNasi, who was frail, suffering and close to death. As the end of his life drew near, his students continued to pray assiduously for their teacher to live. The Talmud records how Rabbi

Yehuda's handmaid, upon seeing the pain and physical discomfort of her master, ascended to the roof of his house and intentionally threw a jar from the roof that shattered as it hit the ground. Startled by the noise, the students were momentarily distracted from their praying, at which time "the soul of Rabbi Yehuda departed to its eternal rest." (BT Ket. 104a) This story is often cited to demonstrate how Judaism does not support extraordinary measures in death care; it also reminds us that sometimes prayer needs to turn from healing of body, to healing of the spirit in preparation for death, and to prayers for the graceful transition of the soul as it leaves the body.

The petitionary prayers of the traditional *Mi Shebeirach* healing ask for a "healing of soul." But what does it mean to pray for "healing of the soul"? Simply put, it means to pray for peace, wholeness, and completion for an individual, whether they live or die. This notion is consistent with Jewish custom: if someone is sick, it is traditional to wish them *"refuah shleimah"*—a Hebrew phrase that translates as "a complete healing." Interestingly, the word, *shleimah,* is a derivative of the Hebrew word, *"shleimut"*—wholeness; similarly, the English word for "healing" is related to the Anglo-Saxon word, *"hal,"* which means to make whole. Thus, to be healed is to become whole. And praying for the "healing of the soul" is a supplication that, even if unable to have a complete physical recovery, a person may be able to experience a sense of inner wholeness, and a connection with the fullness of their soul.

To explore this a bit further: we know from experience with hospice over the past forty years, in addition to physical needs, people who are dying have a wide range of emotional, psycho-social, and spiritual needs.[10] Thus, "healing of the soul" can also be understood as cultivating a sense of wholeness and healing of the emotional, psycho-social, and spiritual dimensions of a person.

In the face of sickness and death, the *emotional needs* of one who is dying consist of being able to find peace within: to forgive themselves for their shortcomings; to see the grand panorama of their life with a sense of equanimity; and ultimately, to transform fear and confusion about dying into a sense of peace, harmony and acceptance.

The *psycho-social needs* for one who is dying is to end life feeling resolution and completion in relationships with the people around them; to let go of old resentments and regrets with family, friends and colleagues; to forgive those who have disappointed them; and to forgive themselves for their shortcomings and inter-personal failings. All of this refers to what Elisabeth Kübler-Ross called "finishing business"—making peace with the various strands of the emotional and psycho-social reality of our lived life.

And further: we know that through the dying process many people—although certainly not all—discover they have deeper *spiritual needs*, having to do with meaning-making, acceptance of death, and spiritual surrender. More specifically, those various spiritual needs encompass (but are not limited to) encountering the existential reality of death; wrestling with finding a deeper meaning and significance to life; feeling finished with the work of this life time; surrendering with spiritual equanimity to the unknown death has in store; and opening up to move on to the next phase of the journey beyond death.

There is no "one size fits all" in arriving at spiritual resolution in the face of death—each person must walk their own journey, and today, the options people chose for meaning-making are varied and multi-dimensional. Whether it is through a traditional path of faith in a religious tradition, a connection with God or spirit, belief or hope in an afterlife or some kind of existence beyond death, a sense of mystical connection with the spirit of the universe, or in a multitude of others ways, ultimately the process of "healing of the soul" allows one to die with acceptance and at peace. In praying for another, we hope our prayers are effective to help a loved one achieve such a state of mind and being at the end of their life.

Prayer as an Anchor to Tradition

The roller coaster ride of life-threatening illness that consists of perplexing symptoms of deteriorating health, trials and tribulations of identification and diagnosis of disease, multiple trips to the hospital for tests and treatments, and the complexity of dealing with the health care and medical insurance system, leaves everyone—patients and their family member care-givers—physically exhausted and emotionally depleted. At those times when the fear of death gnaws silently in the background, evoking intermittent waves of distress and despair, interspersed with hope and heroism, reaching for Jewish tradition can be, for some at least, spiritually comforting and grounding.

The prayers in this book are specifically intended to provide an anchor to the rubrics of Judaism, whether or not one has an extensive background of Jewish knowledge or a familiarity with Jewish practice. Found within these pages are essential prayers of the Jewish tradition: *Shema Yisrael* and the *V'ahavta*; the Priestly Blessing; the traditional *Mi Shebeirach* for healing; Psalm 121; the deathbed confessional or *Vidui*; and other selections which comprise the primary building blocks of Jewish healing practices and deathbed rituals.

Hearing the very sound of these prayers—in Hebrew or English—can have a powerful, grounding effect, connecting a person with the legacy of Judaism, whether in the middle of a highly technological, sometimes dehumanized medical environment, or in the quiet of one's own home.

While there are also newer, contemporary Jewish prayers in this book, many of the Hebrew prayers are ancient, recited by spiritual seekers for millennia. In moments of traditional praying, one might imagine all the generations of people who have recited these words. Images come to mind of all the sons and daughters, husbands and wives who have ever stood next to a dying loved one, praying for their healing, reciting Psalms on their behalf, or escorting their soul as it leaves the body. Ancestral generations of old struggling with the mysteries of life and death were comforted by the resonant words of Jewish prayer. Even with the passing of time, and the development of highly technological contemporary medical settings, traditional Jewish healing prayers continue to have the ability to provide comfort to the heart and a balm for the spirit. It is my hope that both the reader and those hearing the words and melodies of the prayers within this book will be blessed with connection to the strength, wisdom, and mystical power of the Jewish tradition.

Prayer as a Source of Comfort and Connection

Another function of deathbed prayers is to provide comfort and connection for both patients and care-givers who are companioning the dying. As it sometimes turns out, regardless of the ever-expanding array of doctor's deliberations and procedures, the extensive protocols around the use of pharmaceutical potions and concoctions, and the trials and tribulations various traditional and experimental medical options, at some point in the seemingly never-ending journey of patient care, it may well be that death is inevitable. "To everything there is a season, a time to be born, a time to die," and sometimes after months, perhaps years, of medical intervention, it is time to turn from treatment and healing to preparing for death.

Under such circumstances, people who are feeling their own death imminent, and caregivers, supportive family members, as well as professionals involved in chronic, palliative and hospice care, experience a profound vulnerability and powerlessness. As Rabbi Zalman Schachter-Shalomi writes:

> Every one of us has a little space we go to . . . when we are sad, when we feel lonely, when we need to lick our wounds . . . We are the most vulnerable beings when it comes to that space. But that is also the space where we can create a sanctuary for God.[11]

In that vulnerable, liminal space on the edge of death's door, one yearns for comfort, consolation and connection with the divine. As Abraham Joshua Heschel says of those moments of darkness, "we grope for solace, for meaning, for prayer."[12]

In the language of traditional theology, one might say that through prayer one can experience God's comforting presence. Rabbinic and Kabbalistic tradition affirm this notion in the teaching that *Shechinah*, the Divine Presence, is present both at the bedside of one who is sick (BT Ned. 40a), and at the time of a person's death (Zohar III, 88a; Zohar I, 98a). Thus we can say that, aside from the idea of praying for a specific outcome for a sick person, the very act of praying opens one up to be comforted by God's immanent presence, *Shechinah*.

Thus, deathbed prayer is a functional method that acts as a key to the doorway in which we invite God or spirit inside of ourselves. The more time we spend in prayer, the more we deeply attune to that space, the larger that space inside of ourselves. Thus deathbed prayer is also a process of attunement and alignment with *Shechinah*, with divine Presence.

Prayer As Soul-Guiding

One final element of deathbed prayer is what can be called "soul-guiding." If we start with the assumption that consciousness survives bodily death, as Jewish tradition has always held, then the process of dying is one of the soul gently leaving the body. And the work of companioning someone who is dying is to offer loving thoughts while reciting or chanting prayers to escort the soul as it exits the body.

While all the prayers in this book can fulfill this "soul-guiding" function, in particular there are a number of prayers designed specifically for this process. There are different versions of the *Vidui*, the deathbed confession, that can be seen as "soul-guiding" prayers; there are also three different *Vidui* meditations. The goal of these *Vidui* prayers and meditations is to help a person feel resolved in their life and to leave the body behind.

The function of offering soul-guiding prayers is similar to what a midwife does in bringing a child to birth into the world, except soul-guiding on the deathbed aims to help the soul transition more gracefully to the world beyond.

As written in A Techinah for the Deathbed (found in this book):

> As the midwives, Shifra and Puah
> brought forth new life,
> may I help birth this soul
> into the luminosity of the world beyond.

Companioning somebody who is dying is a holy act. May we all be worthy of the calling to escort others in the transition between life and death.

— SIMCHA PAULL RAPHAEL, PH.D.

Shema Yisrael
The Eternal Our God is One

> *Shema Yisrael*, the central prayer of Judaism, affirms our belief that there is One God, and all that we encounter in life is an expression of that One God. The opening line of the *Shema Yisrael* is included in the deathbed *vidui*, and are intended to be the very last words recited by one who is dying.

שְׁמַע יִשְׂרָאֵל, יהוה אֱלֹהֵינוּ, יהוה אֶחָד:

Shema Yisrael,
Adonai Eloheinu,
Adonai Echad.

Hear O Israel:
The Eternal is our God,
The Eternal One Alone!

Baruch Shem Kevod

בָּרוּךְ שֵׁם כְּבוֹד מַלְכוּתוֹ לְעוֹלָם וָעֶד.

Baruch shem kevod malchuto l'olam va'ed!

Blessed be God's ruling Presence
for ever and ever!

V'AHAVTA
AND YOU SHALL LOVE
ADONAI YOUR GOD

THE _V'AHAVTA_ PRAYER is part of the traditional
Shema. It reminds us to open our heart to God,
to spirit. In dealing with the uncertainty of life's
finality, keeping our heart open to God and to the
unknown destiny of life, allows us to open to being
comforted through our own connection with the
divine, with the Source of Life.[13]

וְאָהַבְתָּ אֵת יהוה אֱלֹהֶיךָ, בְּכָל־לְבָבְךָ, וּבְכָל־נַפְשְׁךָ, וּבְכָל־מְאֹדֶךָ:
וְהָיוּ הַדְּבָרִים הָאֵלֶּה, אֲשֶׁר אָנֹכִי מְצַוְּךָ הַיּוֹם, עַל־לְבָבֶךָ: וְשִׁנַּנְתָּם
לְבָנֶיךָ, וְדִבַּרְתָּ בָּם בְּשִׁבְתְּךָ בְּבֵיתֶךָ, וּבְלֶכְתְּךָ בַדֶּרֶךְ וּבְשָׁכְבְּךָ
וּבְקוּמֶךָ: וּקְשַׁרְתָּם לְאוֹת עַל־יָדֶךָ, וְהָיוּ לְטֹטָפֹת בֵּין עֵינֶיךָ:
וּכְתַבְתָּם עַל מְזֻזוֹת בֵּיתֶךָ וּבִשְׁעָרֶיךָ:

V'ahavta et Adonai Elohecha,
b'chol l'vavcha uv'chol nafsh'cha
uv'chol m'odecha.
V'hayu had'varim ha-eileh
asher anochi m'tzav'cha hayom al l'vavecha.
V'shinantam l'vanecha v'dibarta
bam b'shivt'cha b'veitecha uv'lecht'cha

19

vaderech uv'shochb'cha uv'kumecha.
Uk'shartam l'ot al yadecha v'hayu
l'totafot bein einecha. Uch'tavtam
al m'zuzot beitecha uvish'arecha.

You shall love the Eternal, your God,
with all your heart, with all your soul
and with all your might.
And these words
which I command you this day,
shall you take to heart.
Repeat them to your children;
speak of them when you are at home
and when you go out,
when you lie down and when you rise up.
Bind them as a sign upon your hand,
set them as a signet upon your brow.
Write them on the doorposts of your house
and on your gates.

(Deut. 6:5-9)

לְמַעַן תִּזְכְּרוּ וַעֲשִׂיתֶם אֶת־כָּל־מִצְוֹתָי וִהְיִיתֶם קְדֹשִׁים לֵאלֹהֵיכֶם:
אֲנִי יהוה אֱלֹהֵיכֶם אֲשֶׁר הוֹצֵאתִי אֶתְכֶם מֵאֶרֶץ מִצְרַיִם לִהְיוֹת
לָכֶם לֵאלֹהִים אֲנִי יהוה אֱלֹהֵיכֶם:

L'maan tizk'ru, vaasitem et kol mitzvotai
vih'yitem k'doshim l'Eloheichem.
Ani Adonai Eloheichem,
asher hotzeiti et-chem mei-eretz
Mitzrayim lih'yot lachem l'Elohim
ani Adonai Eloheichem.

In order that you remember
to do all my *mitzvot*
and become holy for your God.
I am the Life-giver, your God,
who brought you out of the land of Egypt
to be your God;
I am the Eternal One, your God.

(Num. 15:40-41)

THE PRIESTLY BLESSING

ORIGINALLY FOUND in the Bible (Num. 6:23-27), this prayer was traditionally offered as a blessing upon the people by the priests *(kohanim)* of ancient Israel, and is still in use today in synagogue services, and as part of the *Shabbat* home ritual for blessing of children. It is a prayer which can be recited any time to offer blessings and protection for loved ones.

יְבָרֶכְךָ יהוה וְיִשְׁמְרֶךָ:

יָאֵר יהוה פָּנָיו אֵלֶיךָ וִיחֻנֶּךָ:

יִשָּׂא יהוה פָּנָיו אֵלֶיךָ וְיָשֵׂם לְךָ שָׁלוֹם:

Y'varechecha Adonai veyishmerecha
Ya'er Adonai panav elecha vichuneka.
Yisah Adonai panav elecha veyasem lecha
shalom.

May the blessings of God rest upon you.
May God's peace abide with you.
May God's Presence illuminate your heart,
Now and forever more.

(Trans. Hazrat Inayat Khan)

MI SHEBEIRACH
A Prayer for Healing

THIS IS A VERSION of the traditional Jewish prayer for healing of the sick. In times of illness, if we know physical healing is unlikely, we pray for a healing of the soul and a renewal of the spirit.[14]

מִי שֶׁבֵּרַךְ אֲבוֹתֵינוּ אַבְרָהָם, יִצְחַק, וְיַעֲקֹב

וְאִמּוֹתֵינוּ שָׂרָה, רִבְקָה, רָחֵל וְלֵאָה, הוּא יְבָרֵךְ אֶת

(הַחוֹלֶה \ הַחוֹלָה) _____ (בֶּן \ בַּת) _____ .

הַקָּדוֹשׁ בָּרוּךְ הוּא יִמָּלֵא רַחֲמִים

(עָלָיו, לְהַחֲלִימוֹ וּלְרַפְּאתוֹ וּלְהַחֲזִיקוֹ) \

(עָלֶיהָ, לְהַחֲלִימָהּ וּלְרַפְּאתָהּ וּלְהַחֲזִיקָהּ)

וְיִשְׁלַח (לוֹ \ לָהּ) מְהֵרָה רְפוּאָה שְׁלֵמָה מִן הַשָּׁמַיִם

רְפוּאַת הַנֶּפֶשׁ וּרְפוּאַת הַגּוּף,

הַשְׁתָּא בַּעֲגָלָא וּבִזְמַן קָרִיב וְנֹאמַר אָמֵן.

Mi shebeirach avoteinu:
Avraham, Yitzchak, v'Yaakov,
v'imoteinu: Sarah, Rivka, Rachel v'Leah,
Hu yivarech vyirapei et hacholeh/hacholah
_____ ben/bat _____ .

May the One who blessed our ancestors,
Abraham, Isaac, and Jacob,
Sarah, Rebecca, Rachel, and Leah,
bless and heal the one who is ill:
_____ son/daughter of _____.

May the Holy One, the font of blessings,
shower abundant mercies upon [him/her]
fulfilling [his/her] dreams of healing,
strengthening [him/her]
with the power of life.

Merciful One,
Send [him/her] a complete healing
from the heavenly realm,
a healing of body and a healing of soul,
together with all who are ill,
soon, speedily, without delay.
And let us say: Amen!

B'SHEM HASHEM
ANGEL SONG

THIS PRAYER, with images of the four angelic presences, is found in both the Bedtime Shema, and the traditional deathbed *Vidui* or confessional. English translation by Rabbi Geela Rayzel Raphael. For musical rendition, see Geela Rayzel Raphael, *May the Angels Carry You - Jewish Songs of Comfort for Death, Dying and Mourning*, www.shechinah.com.

בְּשֵׁם ה', בְּשֵׁם ה',
אֱלֹהֵי יִשְׂרָאֵל
מִימִינִי מִיכָאֵל
וּמִשְׂמֹאלִי גַּבְרִיאֵל
וּמִלְפָנַי אוּרִיאֵל
וּמֵאֲחוֹרַי רְפָאֵל
וְעַל רֹאשִׁי וְעַל רֹאשִׁי
שְׁכִינַת אֵל.

B'shem HaShem,
B'shem HaShem,
Elohei Yisrael.
Mi'yimini Michael,
umi'smoli Gabriel,
Mi'lifnai Uriel,
umi'achorai Raphael.
Ve'al roshi,
ve'al roshi Shechinat El

In the name of God,
the God of Israel.
There is Michael and Gabriel,
Uriel and Raphael,
the four of them they gather
and dance around your soul,
and the Shechinah Herself appears
to make your spirit whole.

Gesher Tzar Me'od
A Very Narrow Bridge

This song is based upon a saying by the Hasidic Rebbe, Nahman of Bratslav. These words remind us to keep our hearts open in the face of fear and life's unforeseen transitions.

כָּל הָעוֹלָם כֻּלּוֹ

גֶּשֶׁר צַר מְאֹד

וְהָעִקָּר, וְהָעִקָּר

לֹא לְפַחֵד, לֹא לְפַחֵד כְּלָל.

Kol ha-olam kulo
Gesher tzar me'od (2x)
Kol ha-olam kulo
Gesher tzar me'od (2x)
V'ha-ikar, V'ha-ikar
Lo l'facheyd, lo l'facheyd klal.

The whole world
is just a narrow bridge,
just a narrow bridge;

and the most,
the most important thing,
is to have no fear at all.

PSALM 121
A SONG OF ASCENTS

PSALM 121 is part of the Shabbat morning service. Reciting this Psalm reminds us we are protected and watched over at all times.[15]

שִׁיר לַמַּעֲלוֹת אֶשָּׂא עֵינַי אֶל־הֶהָרִים מֵאַיִן יָבֹא עֶזְרִי:
עֶזְרִי מֵעִם יהוה עֹשֵׂה שָׁמַיִם וָאָרֶץ:

Esah einai el heharim, ma'ayin yavoh ezri?
Ezri me'im HaShem oseh shamayim
  va'aretz.

I lift my eyes up to the mountains;
from where does my help come?
My help comes the Eternal,
maker of heaven and earth,
who will not let your foot stumble;
your guardian who will not slumber.

Behold the guardian of Israel
neither slumbers nor sleeps.
The Eternal is your guardian;

the Everpresent,
your protection at your right side.
The sun will not smite you by day,
nor the moon by night;
the Everpresent guards you from all evil,
guards your very being.
The Eternal guards your going out and
coming in, now and forever.

VIDUI
A PRAYER OF TRANSITION

Recited by One Who is Dying

THE *VIDUI* is a prayer of transition for the deathbed. This version of the *Vidui*, recited by one who is gravely ill, is designed to help the person who is dying to peacefully accept the finality of life's end.[16]

יי אֱלֹהַי, רְפוּאָתִי וּמִיתָתִי בְּיָדֶךָ.

יְהִי רָצוֹן מִלְּפָנֶיךָ, שֶׁתִּרְפָּאֵנִי רְפוּאָה שְׁלֵמָה.

אֲבִי יְתוֹמִים וְדַיַּן אַלְמָנוֹת, הָגֵן בְּעַד קְרוֹבַי הַיְקָרִים אֲשֶׁר נַפְשִׁי

קְשׁוּרָה בְּנַפְשָׁם. בְּיָדְךָ אַפְקִיד רוּחִי פָּדִיתָ אוֹתִי יי אֵל אֱמֶת אָמֵן

וְאָמֵן.

שְׁמַע יִשְׂרָאֵל, יהוה אֱלֹהֵינוּ, יהוה אֶחָד:

בָּרוּךְ שֵׁם כְּבוֹד מַלְכוּתוֹ לְעוֹלָם וָעֶד.

יי מֶלֶךְ, יי מָלָךְ, יי יִמְלוֹךְ לְעוֹלָם וָעֶד.

יי הוּא הָאֱלֹהִים. יי הוּא הָאֱלֹהִים.

I acknowledge before the Source of All
that life and death are not in my hands.

33

Just as I did not choose to be born,
so I do not choose to die.

May it come to pass that I may be healed,
but if death is my fate,
then I accept it with dignity
and the loving calm
of one who knows the way of all things.

May my death be honorable,
and may my life be a healing memory
for those who know me.

May my loved ones think well of me,
and may my memory bring them joy.

For all those I may have hurt,
I ask forgiveness.
Upon all who have hurt me,
I bestow forgiveness.
As a wave returns to the ocean,
so I return to the Source from which I came.

Shema Yisrael, Adonai Eloheinu,
Adonai Echad!

Hear O Israel,
that which we call God is Oneness itself.
Blessed is the Way of God,

the Way of Life and Death,
of coming and going,
of meeting and loving,
now and forever.
As I was blessed with the one
so now I am blessed with the other.
Shalom. Shalom. Shalom.

VIDUI
A PRAYER OF TRANSITION

Recited on Behalf of
One Who is Dying

WHEN A DYING person is gravely ill, this version of the *Vidui* prayer of transition is recited on their behalf, and within range of their hearing.[17]

מוֹדִים אֲנַחְנוּ לָךְ יי אֱלֹהֵינוּ וֵאלֹהֵי אֲבוֹתֵינוּ וְאִמּוֹתֵינוּ, שֶׁחַיֵּינוּ מְסוּרִים בְּיָדֶךָ. יְהִי רָצוֹן מִלְּפָנֶיךָ, שֶׁתְּרַפֵּא אֶת (הַחוֹלֶה הַמְסֻכָּן הַזֶּה \ הַחוֹלָה הַמְסֻכָּנָה הַזֹּאת) רְפוּאָה שְׁלֵמָה. וְאִם הַמָּוֶת כָּלָה וְנֶחֱרַץ מֵעִמְּךָ, (יְקָחֵנוּ \ יְקָחֶהָ) מִיָּדְךָ בְּאַהֲבָה. וּתְהִי (מִיתָתוֹ \ מִיתָתָהּ) כַּפָּרָה עַל כָּל חֲטָאִים וַעֲוֹנוֹת וּפְשָׁעִים, (שֶׁחָטָא וְשֶׁעָוָה וְשֶׁפָּשַׁע \ שֶׁחָטְאָה וְשֶׁעָוְתָה וְשֶׁפָּשְׁעָה) לְפָנֶיךָ. וְתַשְׁפִּיעַ (לוֹ \ לָהּ) מֵרַב טוֹב הַצָּפוּן לַצַּדִּיקִים (וְתוֹדִיעֵהוּ \ וְתוֹדִיעֶהָ) אֹרַח חַיִּים.

37

אֲבִי יְתוֹמִים וְדַיַּן אַלְמָנוֹת, הָגֵן בְּעַד (קְרוֹבָיו \ קְרוֹבֶיהָ) הַיְקָרִים
אֲשֶׁר (נַפְשׁוֹ \ נַפְשָׁהּ) קְשׁוּרָה בְּנַפְשָׁם.
בְּיָדְךָ (יַפְקִיד רוּחוֹ \ תַּפְקִיד רוּחָהּ) פָּדִיתָ (אוֹתוֹ \ אוֹתָהּ)
יי אֵל אֱמֶת אָמֵן וְאָמֵן.

שְׁמַע יִשְׂרָאֵל, יהוה אֱלֹהֵינוּ, יהוה אֶחָד:
בָּרוּךְ שֵׁם כְּבוֹד מַלְכוּתוֹ לְעוֹלָם וָעֶד.
יי מֶלֶךְ, יי מָלָךְ, יי יִמְלוֹךְ לְעוֹלָם וָעֶד.
יי הוּא הָאֱלֹהִים. יי הוּא הָאֱלֹהִים.

Shema Yisrael, Adonai Eloheinu,
Adonai Echad (7x)
Baruch Shem Kevod Malchuto
L'olam Vaed (3x)
Adonai Melech, Adonai Malach,
Adonai Yimloch L'olam Vaed (3x)
Adonai Hu Ha-Elohim (7x)

Adonai, our God, and God of our ancestors, We acknowledge that all life is in your hands. May it be Your will to send healing to _____.

Yet if the end is imminent, may it reflect Your love and atone for all those times _____ could have done better.

Grant [him/her] the rewards of the righteous, and give [him/her] eternal life in your Presence.

Guardian of the bereaved, protect _____ and [his/her] beloved family, for their lives are interconnected in the bond of love.

In your hand lives [his/her] spirit. You have redeemed [him/her], *Adonai*, God of Truth.

Hear O Israel, *Adonai* is our God, *Adonai* is One.

Through Time and Space Your Glory Shines, Our Blessed One.

> *Adonai* reigns, *Adonai* has reigned,
> *Adonai* shall reign forever and ever.
> *Adonai* is God, *Adonai* is God.

A *Techinah* for
the Deathbed

Techinot (sing., *Techinah*) are personal women's prayers, originally written in Yiddish in the Jewish communities of Eastern Europe. The tradition of women's prayers—often for birth, pregnancy, mourning and other concerns of women's lives—dates back to the 1600s. This contemporary *Techinah* prayer was written by Rabbi Geela Rayzel and Reb Simcha Raphael. For a musical rendition, see Geela Rayzel Raphael, *May the Angels Carry You: Jewish Songs of Comfort for Death, Dying and Mourning*.

O Great Guardian of the Gateway
between life and death,
I come before you as witness
to this sacred moment in time.
In gratitude and with humility
I honor the mystery of holy transition.

Just as Jacob buried his beloved Rachel
on the road to Bethlehem,
and as loving family surrounded
Jacob and Joseph

as they were gathered to their ancestors,
may I gracefully escort the soul of _____
with compassionate love.
As the midwives, Shifra and Puah
brought forth new life,
may I help birth this soul
into the luminosity of the world beyond.

O Holy One of Blessing,
may I be a comforting presence
for all those gathered here.
Grant me the wisdom
to speak gentle words,
to sing sacred songs,
and to be silent in the face of the unknown.
Give me an open heart and presence of mind
for this divine unfolding.

Majesty of Time and Space,
send guardians and guides,
ancestors and angels
to accompany this soul
on its homeward journey.
Michael, Gabriel, Uriel, and Raphael,
please safeguard the passage
between the lower and upper worlds.
As the breath wanes
and the body is released,
O Holy *Shechinah*,

carry this soul on your shimmering wings into the radiant light of *Gan Eden.*

As the spirit of life is extinguished, we pray:

Shema Yisrael, Adonai Eloheinu,
Adonai Echad (3x).

Exercise
Writing One's Personal *Vidui*

THE GOAL OF THIS EXERCISE, created by Rabbi
Nadya Gross, is to imagine what one would want
to have as the last words upon their deathbed, and
create a personally-written deathbed confession
which can be read back to a person in the final
moments of life. It can be done by someone
dealing with sickness and end-of-life concerns, or
by a care-giver for another person wrestling with
the approach of death. When written out, this
personal *vidui* can can be used in addition to, or in
place of a traditional *vidui*.

Introduction
Creating a Personal *Vidui*

A powerful tool in counseling and pastoral
work with the dying is the process of writing
one's own *Vidui*. Discussing and writing
responses to the questions below are profoundly
effective ways to make meaning out of the life
one has lived, to distill life down to the most
precious achievements and relationships, and
to clear away obstacles that stand in the way of

complete surrender to the inevitable. Writing one's own deathbed prayer serves as a means to confront the truth of one's life, and invites one to consciously enter into the Presence of the Holy One as death approaches.

Here are some possible elements to consider in writing a *Vidui* (though you should also feel free to add and improvise):

Who Is My God?

In writing your *Vidui*, think about to whom you are presenting yourself. The opening phrase of the traditional *Vidui* addresses God—"*Adonai,* our God, and God of our ancestors." What is the nature of your own relationship with God? To whom are you entrusting your soul as you prepare to transition from this life into the next? Is this the "God of my ancestors," the "Source of Life and Breath," the "Beloved," or something other? How do you choose to speak with God in prayer?

Who Am I?

What have been the accomplishments of your life that you are proud of? What have been the meaningful relationships of your life? Completing this part of the *Vidui,* adding the personal content missing from the traditional deathbed prayer, brings the reality of your life into focus, narrating in brief (or extensively) those aspects of life that provided meaning and purpose. It also opens for you the possibility of being able to rest in the comfort of knowing that there will be residual and relevant traces of your life shared with those left behind.

Regrets?

Think about what might have been life undone, regrets that you have. Whenever life comes to an end, there are always regrets and a sense of tasks not completed, 'conversations left in the middle of a sentence.' Naming these makes it easier to let go.

Prayers for Those Left Behind

What is your prayer, what are your wishes for those you leave behind? Your ability to let go may depend on knowing that the ones you leave behind will continue to thrive. As you anticipate crossing the threshold, imagine the many blessings that your loved ones will yet experience as their lives go on.

A Statement of Surrender or Gratitude

Are there final words of surrender or gratitude you want to include in your *Vidui?* Can you imagine how you might be greeted on the other side?

MAY THE ANGELS CARRY YOU
A *VIDUI* SONG

THIS SONG by Rabbi Geela Rayzel Raphael is based upon elements of the traditional *Vidui* prayer. For the music, see Geela Rayzel Raphael, *May the Angels Carry You: Jewish Songs of Comfort for Death, Dying and Mourning.*

At this time of transition, going to the light
At this time of transition, going home is right
Let go of the struggle, let go of your fear
All will be forgiven, your slate to be cleared.

CHORUS: May the angels carry you (2x)

Your work is done, it is time to rest
The fruit of your hands and your soul be blessed
Joining your ancestors, finding a new way
Crossing the threshold, wrapped in God's
            embrace.

CHORUS: May the angels carry you (2x)

Surrounded by love, angels take your hand
Guiding you on, its part of the plan

Shechinah welcomes you opening her wings
Hearing the chorus, join the angels singing.

CHORUS: May the angels carry you (2x)

Mi'yimini Michaella
Mi'smoli Gavriella
Mi'lifnai Uriella
U mi'achorai Raphaella

CHORUS: May the angels carry you (2x)

VIDUI MEDITATIONS
OF TRANSITION

WHAT FOLLOWS is a series of three meditations based upon images found in the traditional *Vidui* prayer, the Jewish deathbed confession.[18]

The practice of using guided visualizations for one who is dying is derived, in part, from a synthesis of humanistic and transpersonal psychology and Tibetan Buddhism. Both Humanistic and Transpersonal psychology emerged in the late 1960's as a psychological approach to actualizing the higher spiritual potentialities of the individual, and developed a methodology using experiential visualizations to explore inner realms of consciousness. Tibetan Buddhism—known for the text, *Bardo Thodol*, what is generally translated, *The Tibetan Book of the Dead*, dating from the 1600's—cultivated a practice of reading the words of a sacred text to guide the post-mortem being on a journey of transformation and awakening.[19] These meditations were created as a way of enabling a person who is dying—whether conscious or unconscious—to prepare for their own departure from the physical world.

In advance of using these *Vidui* meditations with someone nearing death, it is important to familiarize yourself with them first. Take time to read aloud each one of the meditations slowly, acquainting yourself with the nuances of the words and metaphors. As you read with unhurried concentration, breathe slowly and deeply, and notice the movement of your own breathing.

As a guide for someone embarking on the journey of dying, be present not only with the words, but also inwardly, in your own awareness. Offering a guided meditation for one who is dying is itself a contemplative process. Before you begin to read, align yourself with the spirit of the person with whom you are sitting, and pay attention to the inner thoughts and feelings which emerge. Trust your intuition.

The reading of these meditations is not a science, but an art, it is an art of human connection. You are engaged in what may be described as "soul-guiding." These are meditations to help the process of the soul leaving behind the body. As you read slowly and with intention, allow the words, the gentle rhythm of your own breathing, and your own heart to help you connect with the soul of the person who is before you. If possible, play soft, contemplative music in the background. Just because someone is asleep, unconscious or comatose, does not mean that you cannot connect with them inwardly. Even in an unconscious state, people nearing death have an uncanny way of sensing the presence of a loved one who is with them. Continue to speak with them: remember this is sacred time, and you are a midwife to the departing soul.

You can choose to use any of these meditations, and they can be repeated multiple times.

1. *Vidui Meditation*
Purification/Opening to the World Beyond

My dear beloved *[name in English and Hebrew]*, at this time of transition, your body is losing strength and the energy to maintain its connection with the life force. You are beginning to experience the process of slowly dissolving out of that body. As a butterfly leaves behind a cocoon, you are leaving the physical body behind, entering a whole other realm of experience. You are about to be welcomed into the world beyond. As this happens, you will notice a series of images, visions, and memories. Do not be afraid; you are safe, you are protected.

As you prepare to leave behind the physical body, you may have memories emerging of living your life in a physical body, you may have memories of the challenges and struggles you have had with health and well-being in recent weeks and months. Simply notice all of those images and memories of bodily struggle, and let them all go. Allow all the pains and challenges of the body to be washed away in a river of divine light. You can let go.

Now, you may notice many different feelings emerging, memories from life-experience. You may notice feeling memories of sadness and joy, of the struggles and the blessings of life. Simply notice any or all those memories. Allow all those feeling-memories to be washed away in a river of divine light. You can let go.

You may notice many thoughts emerging now. You may see different memory-experiences of your life. You may see a vision of everything you have ever done, or perhaps a replaying of the story of your life from beginning to end. Simply notice the memories of that story called your life. Allow all those memories of that story to be washed away in a river of divine light. You can let go.

Now allow yourself to be transported to a new realm, seeing yourself as a fledgling bird transported by the wings of a majestic eagle. Feel yourself carried towards lofty celestial regions. Sense the winds transporting your consciousness, carrying your soul towards a luxurious and fragrant garden. As you approach this garden, notice all the beauty and radiance surrounding you.

Now glance beyond the garden and see that there are gates opening for you. Sense yourself entering these gates, noticing the many holy beings present with you there. You are being welcomed to the world beyond, you are being blessed and carried by God's loving presence. You are protected from the negativity of any distracting thoughts. Feel your soul encased in a luminescent globe of loving protection. You are being welcomed into the world beyond. Surrender ever and ever more deeply . . . God is guarding and protecting your exit from this world and your entry into the world beyond. Feeling your soul surrounded light, you are safe, you are loved, you are free to let go anytime you are ready.

2. *Vidui Meditation*
Invoking the Angels

IT IS TAUGHT in the Zohar: *"No one dies before he or she sees the Shechinah . . .* (Zohar III, 88a) *and along with the Shechinah there come... [accompanying] ministering angels to receive the soul of the departed one."* (Zohar I, 98a) Jewish tradition teaches there are angelic presences who are there to accompany beings in their time of transition. This meditation uses the images of the four guardian angels.

My dear beloved *[name in English and Hebrew]*, at this time of transition, you are not alone. I am here with you as a loving guide, and you are also being guided by divine angels accompanying you on your journey to the world beyond. As you hear my words, allow your mind to embrace whatever images emerge; notice them and be aware of their significance for your life. Allow yourself to be open to all that is passing through your consciousness; there is nothing to fear. You are protected and guided at every moment. Remain open. You are safe. You are not alone.

Allow yourself to focus on the very center of your being. Attune to the center of your consciousness. Observe what is happening in this moment; do not be distracted by all that is peripheral. Simply notice all you observe, allowing your breathing to be slow and gentle. Continue to relax. Focus ever and ever more deeply on the center, the source of your own consciousness.

Now allow yourself to connect with the loving Presence of *Shechinah,* God's Presence, the source of all life. Feel that connection, bask in it. Go closer. Remember you are protected and guided.

Notice to your right a luminescent angelic being, a spiritual force field radiating love and compassion. This is *Michael, the Angel of Compassion.* Connect with this being. Feel its presence. Know that you are protected and guided with the angel Michael at your right.

Now notice to your left a luminescent angelic being, a spiritual force field radiating strength and power. This is *Gabriel, the Angel of Strength.* Connect with this being. Feel its presence. Know that you are protected and guided with the angel Gabriel at your left.

Notice in front of you a luminescent angelic being, a spiritual force field radiating soft light. This is *Uriel, the Angel of Light*. Connect with this being. Feel its presence. Know that you are protected and guided with angel Uriel in front of you.

Now, notice behind you a luminescent angelic being, a spiritual force field radiating healing. This is *Raphael, the Angel of Healing*. Connect with this being. Feel its presence... Know that you are protected and guided with the angel Raphael behind you.

Notice above your head the *Divine Presence of Shechinah* enveloping you in a spiritual force field of loving protection. This is *Shechinat El*, the loving *Shechinah* Herself. Connect with this being. Feel its presence. Know that you are protected and guided with the holy *Shechinah* above your head.

Notice all these angelic beings surrounding you, enveloping your entire being. Open to this experience. Feel your soul being welcomed home. Sense the presence of these angelic beings and any others who may be present for you at this time. Communicate with them and receive the messages they have for you. Observe all that is happening. There is nothing to fear, you are safe, you are protected, you are loved. You are safe, you are protected, you are loved.

3. *Vidui Meditation*
Letting Go of the Physical Body

My dear beloved [name in English and Hebrew], your time to leave this world is rapidly approaching. You are getting ready to leave behind familiar surroundings, and all the ordinary material and physical things you accumulated and accomplished in this lifetime. The slow transition we call dying is taking place. Now is the time for you to prepare to say goodbye to and leave behind the physical body that has known so much illness and suffering.

As I speak, hear the words I am saying, and allow them to enter your consciousness fully. There is nothing to fear; you are not alone. I am with you in this moment, and soon you will be welcomed into the world beyond by loving, caring beings you have known. The has time come to let go of the body, just as a butterfly leaves behind the cocoon of the caterpillar. You are safe, you are protected, there is nothing to fear. Notice all that is happening around and inside of you. You are safe, you are protected, there is nothing to fear.

My dear beloved [name in English and Hebrew], know that in your life you have done the best you have been able to do. You have loved and given love. Now is the time to forgive yourself and know that you are forgiven for everything. Your loved ones are now able to let you go and will be able to manage without you. Now is the time to allow yourself to let go, to relax, and open to what is happening in this moment. Your soul, your consciousness, your energy is preparing to leave behind the physical body. Feel yourself slowly dissolving out of the body, knowing there is nothing to fear, nothing to resist, nothing to cling to. You are safe, you are protected, you are loved. You are safe, you are protected, you are loved. Feel yourself slowly dissolving out of the body and being welcomed into the world beyond, being welcomed by the *Shechinah*, God's loving Presence.

The following words can be sung or chanted, in any melody:

בָּרוּךְ שֵׁם כְּבוֹד מַלְכוּתוֹ לְעוֹלָם וָעֶד.

יי מֶלֶךְ, יי מָלָךְ, יי יִמְלוֹךְ לְעוֹלָם וָעֶד.

יי הוּא הָאֱלֹהִים. יי הוּא הָאֱלֹהִים.

שְׁמַע יִשְׂרָאֵל, יהוה אֱלֹהֵינוּ, יהוה אֶחָד:

Baruch Shem Kevod
Malchuto L'olam Vaed (3x)
Adonai Melech, Adonai Malach,
Adonai Yimloch L'olam Vaed (3x)
Adonai Hu Ha-Elohim (7x)
Shema Yisrael, Adonai Eloheinu,
Adonai Echad (7x)

A Prayer for When Life Support Is Being Removed

This prayer written by Rabbinic Pastor Stephanie Tivona Reith is for those moments when a difficult and painful decision has been made to remove life support for a family member. The prayer allows for a sanctification of the moment when the dying loved one is in a hyper-medicalized environment. The words are designed to bring comfort and spiritual understanding to this end-of-life setting.

Oh Holy and Eternal God,
we stand now before You,
our hearts breaking.

For the last few days,
we have stood by our beloved _____,
and have been witness to his/her
struggle for life.

We thank you
for the good and loving work
of the doctors and nurses
who have cared for him/her.

We also thank you
for the medicines and machinery
that have allowed _____
to remain in this world with us.

But we know this would not be a struggle
he/she would want to continue in this way.

And so now,
as these medical machines are withdrawn,
we humbly entrust the life of _____
into Your hands.

If it be Your will that he/she live,
please send him/her a perfect healing.

And if it be Your will that he/she
be taken by death, we pray you,
let it be with dignity, free of pain,
and in love.

In life and in death,
we pray that You watch over
the soul of _____,
and help him/her find his/her way
to forgiveness, peace, and everlasting life.

We also pray that you
be with all of us in this room,

to hold us up during this time of anguish,
to mend our broken hearts,
and to comfort us as we grieve
this beloved soul.

In your Holy Name,
Amen.

ANA B'KOACH
SOURCE OF MERCY

A TRADITIONAL Friday night *Shabbat* prayer that petitions God to bless us and hear our prayers. Translation by Rabbi Zalman Schachter-Shalomi, z"l. This may be recited at any time.

אָנָּא, בְּכֹחַ גְּדֻלַּת יְמִינְךָ תַּתִּיר צְרוּרָה:

קַבֵּל רִנַּת עַמְּךָ, שַׂגְּבֵנוּ, טַהֲרֵנוּ, נוֹרָא:

נָא גִבּוֹר, דּוֹרְשֵׁי יִחוּדְךָ כְּבָבַת שָׁמְרֵם:

בָּרְכֵם, טַהֲרֵם, רַחֲמֵי צִדְקָתְךָ תָּמִיד גָּמְלֵם:

חֲסִין קָדוֹשׁ, בְּרוֹב טוּבְךָ נַהֵל עֲדָתֶךָ:

יָחִיד גֵּאֶה, לְעַמְּךָ פְּנֵה, זוֹכְרֵי קְדֻשָּׁתֶךָ:

שַׁוְעָתֵנוּ קַבֵּל וּשְׁמַע צַעֲקָתֵנוּ, יוֹדֵעַ תַּעֲלוּמוֹת:

Source of Mercy!
With loving strength
Untie our tangles.

Your chanting folk
rise high, make pure.
Accept our song.

Like your own eye
Lord keep us safe
Who union seek.

Cleanse and bless us,
Infuse us ever
With loving care.

Gracious source
Of holy power!
Do guide your folk.

Sublime and holy One,
Do to turn to us,
Of holy chant.

Receive our prayer,
Do hear our cry,
Who secrets knows.

Through time and space
Your glory shines
Our blessed One.

Baruch shem kevod malchuto l'olam va'ed.

LIFE REVIEW, LEGACY, AND WORDS OF COMFORT

Conversation Starters with Someone on an End-of-Life Journey

1. What were the highlights of your life— growing up, as a child and teenager? Your early adult life? Middle age? And recent years?

2. Are there any specific memories you want to talk about right now?

3. Who were the important influences on your life?

4. Do you have any regrets in life you want to talk about?

5. How do you want me/us to remember you?

6. What do you want your legacy to me/us to be?

7. Is there something that is incomplete or unfinished of your life's work?

8. Are there things I/we can do to help complete or fulfill this work for you?

9. What are your wishes and blessings for those you are leaving?

10. Who do you imagine being there to greet you on the other side?[20]

Words of Comfort for One Who is Dying

1. You are loved and you are forgiven.

2. We know you did your very best.

3. You are not going to be alone. We will be with you here, and you will be welcomed by loved ones on the other side.

4. Whenever you are ready, it's okay to leave. We will all be okay.[21]

PONDERING THE MYSTERIES OF LIFE AND DEATH

As daylight wanes
The darkness of dusk permeates and
  pervades
The late autumn sky
Signaling a slow but significant
Imminent and obvious approach of winter.
And I, an aging adult child of mother and
  father
Sit prayerfully, lingering in this liminal
  time zone
Knowing one who is beloved to me
Lies languishing in a hospice hospital bed
Dreaming and drifting off to yonder realms
Of ancient ancestors and archetypal beings
Who wondrously and willingly welcome
  ascending souls
To the little-known and unknown nether
  realms of the world beyond.

In a twilight zone
Of quiet contemplative silence I sit

Pensively pondering rapidly shifting
   realities
Seeing ever-so-clearly the subtle cycles of
   time
The circle of life and death, birth and
   rebirth
Unceasing change and transition.
From deep within distant, dormant caverns
   of psyche and soul
I notice waves of grief, anguish and pain
   emerge
Interwoven and intermingled into the
   fabric of oh so many
Recalled images of eons past
Tender and tantalizing memory moments
Of love and longing
Of yesterday and yesteryears
Of youthful yearning
And midlife meandering.
Remembering the past of what once was
And at one and the same time
Realizing with grief-struck awe
The future that will never be.

In the interior crevices and crevasses of my
   soul
These never-ending crescendos and waves
Of time, memory and meaning
Emerge and converge in this moment

And this moment
And this moment.
Each so powerful, so sacred, so transient.

As daytime definitely disappears
And nightfall noticeably manifests
Somehow silently sneaking up on me
My reflective somnambulant mood changes
Becoming one of fearful and fear-filled
   uncertainty
Of what the very next moment will bring.
My mind wanders from here to there and
   back
As I wonder in unending anxious
   anticipation
If all the medical technology money can
   buy
Can keep alive embodied souls
Who seem to have lived out their divinely
   allotted destiny.

When does daylight officially become night?
In this twilight zone of liminal time
Between sun pattern and star pattern
Is there life or death?
Are we in yesterday or tomorrow?
Beloved being of embodied life
Now and forever finely fading away
Being carefully caressed back to God

Is there anywhere else to go?
Is there any better time than now?

And as for me, in my pained mental
    meandering
I wonder if perhaps my solution and
    resolution
To this emotional discord might be just to
    go to sleep
Turn off my incessantly anxious mind
Rest my hurting heart
Restore my weary body
And maybe, just maybe
I can wake up on the other side of this
    darkness
Wake up in bright sunlight
Love
Life
Joy
Vitality
Does night time take that away?
Is Death a destroyer of All?
Or only a slight shift from what is
Back towards the One?
Towards the truth of life's mystery.

— SIMCHA PAULL RAPHAEL

Afterlife Journey
of the Soul in Kabbalah

While many are often unaware Judaism upholds a belief in an afterlife, in ancient and medieval times there was never any question about whether or not there was life after death. For those living in pre-modern times, between the world of the living and the world of the dead there was a window, not a wall. Those beings who had died continued to stay in contact with beloved family members as benevolent beings, spirit guides and intercessors who could watch over the living offering guidance and blessing. Death was regarded as a transition from the realm of life to the world beyond, and the afterlife was seen as a multi-phased journey of transformation for the soul.

In Jewish mysticism, specifically Kabbalah—a Jewish mystical movement which developed extensively in the 12th to 16th centuries—we find a series of teachings on the afterlife which expanded earlier ideas about life after death notions originally articulated in Torah, and later in Talmud and Midrash. Since beliefs about afterlife were not systematized or codified, Kabbalistic afterlife teachings form a panoramic pastiche of images, a descriptive cartography of ever-changing visionary phenomena and states of consciousness encountered at the moment of bodily death, and in the world beyond.

In Zohar—a Kabbalistic commentary on the Torah written in the late 12th-century—the post-mortem journey is conceived as a four-fold process of: separation from the physical realm; emotional cleansing; transcendent awareness; and ultimately divine union. Terms used to describe these processes are: *Hibbut Ha-Kever*, pangs of the grave as one departs the physical realm; *Gehenna*, a state of emotional purification and purgation; *Gan Eden*, the heavenly Garden of Eden, a realm of transcendent divine recompense; and *Tzror Ha-Hayyim*, a return to the Source of Life wherein the highest level of soul qualities merge with the divine.

Hibbut Ha-Kever
The "Pangs of the Grave"

The first phase of the afterlife journey in Kabbalistic sources is *Hibbut Ha-Kever*, "pangs of the grave." It is depicted as a three to seven day process of separation of the soul from the physical body. During this time, the disembodied being undergoes a purification process surrendering attachments to the physical realm. The task for the dying is to gracefully let go of the physical plane of life and embodiment. For those beings who have cultivated spiritual awareness, leaving behind the physical body and material existence can be painless, effortless, "like drawing a hair out of milk" (BT Ber. 8a). However, if one is clinging to physical existence, the process of separation can be excruciatingly painful. The disembodied soul "wanders about the world and beholds the body which was once its home devoured by worms and suffering the judgment of the grave [*Hibbut Ha-Kever*]" (Zohar II, 141b-142a).

There is a correlation between the length of *Hibbut Ha-Kever*, and the Jewish ritual of *Shiva,* as the Zohar indicates: "For seven days the soul goes to and fro from his house to his grave from his grave to his house, mourning for the body." (Zohar I, 218b). What this suggests is that, in the time immediately after death, the soul of the deceased person can stay in close proximity to the physical world. In this period of time, people often have a felt sense of the presence of the deceased, as well as meaningful synchronistic experiences in which one feels a sense of connection with deceased loved ones.

In early phases of the afterlife journey, the

disembodied soul experiences a variety of visionary experiences. The Zohar describes how ancestral beings and angelic guides escort the soul from the time of death onwards: "At the hour of a man's departure from the world, his father and his relatives gather round him, and he sees them and recognizes them, and likewise all with whom he associated in this world, and they accompany his soul to the place where it is to abide" (Zohar I, 218a). Elsewhere, the Zohar asserts that: "No man leaves the world before he sees the *Shechinah* . . . (Zohar III, 88a) and with the *Shechinah* there come three ministering angels to receive the soul of the righteous" (Zohar I, 98a). Another vision depicted is a life review: "When God desires to take back a man's spirit, all the days that he lived in this world pass before him in review" (Zohar I, 221b). These various post-mortem visions all parallel reports from contemporary near-death experiences.

Gehenna
Emotional Purgation and Purification

The second phase of the afterlife journey is a state of purgation known as *Gehenna*, or *Gehinnom*. As developed within the moral, ethical worldview of the Rabbis, *Gehenna* was an abode of torment for the wicked who have forsaken God and Torah. Medieval Kabbalah adopted this view, but understood *Gehenna* psycho-spiritually as a process of cleansing and transforming incomplete, unresolved emotional residue of life-experience. According to Zohar: "... whoever pollutes himself in the world draws to himself the spirit of uncleanness, and when his soul leaves him the unclean spirits pollute it, and its habitation is among them" (Zohar II, 129b).

This cleansing process of *Gehenna* is described as purification by fire: "In *Gehenna* there are certain places [where] souls that have been polluted by the filth of this world . . . are purified by fire and made white." (Zohar II, 150b). Fire is utilized to punish souls because it represents the quality of human passion: "The fire of *Gehenna*, which burns day and night, corresponds to the hot passion of sinfulness in man" (Zohar II, 150b). The greater one's unbridled passion (usually implying sexuality), the more intensely the fire burns. Thus, the soul's *Gehenna* experience reflects the impurities accumulated during one's lifetime. The more defiled, the greater the need for fires of purification: "When a man's sins are so numerous that he has to pass through the nethermost compartments of *Gehenna* in order to receive heavier punishment corresponding to the contamination of his soul, a more intense fire is kindled in order to consume that contamination (Zohar II, 212a).

Adopting Rabbinic tradition (BT Shab. 33b), Kabbalists affirmed that purification in *Gehenna* was to be endured for a maximum of twelve months, after which time the soul transits to higher afterlife realms (Zohar I, 107a-108a). The ritual practice of children reciting the Mourners' Kaddish for a deceased parent emerged in medieval times, and was regarded as a spiritually efficacious practice for redeeming the soul from the torments of *Gehenna*. Rabbi Moses ben Israel Isserles (1525-1572) limited recitation of the Mourners' Kaddish for parents to eleven months. According to Isserles, since twelve months was maximum time for a soul in *Gehenna*, one would not want to assume one's dead parents deserved full punishment.

When the purification of *Gehenna* ends, the soul is ready to enter other phases of afterlife sojourning. As Zohar teaches: "The body is punished in the grave and the soul in the fire of *Gehinnom* for the appointed period. When this is completed she rises from *Gehinnom* purified of her guilt like iron purified in the fire, and she is carried up to the *Gan Eden*" (Zohar, III, 53a).

Gan Eden
The Heavenly Garden of Eden

The third phase of the afterlife journey is described as *Gan Eden*, the heavenly Garden of Eden, where souls of the righteous dwell. Depicted in mythic images of beauty and bliss in Midrashic tradition (Yalkut Shimoni, Bereshit 20), in medieval Kabbalah, *Gan Eden* is essentially a period of intellectual contemplation of supernal bliss, experienced by the transcendent dimensions of soul. Eternal in nature, the cleansed soul in the heavenly *Gan Eden* experiences a state of consciousness reflecting the level of spiritual development attained during life: ". . . when the soul mounts on high through that portal of the firmament [i.e. to the heavenly *Gan Eden*], other precious garments are provided for it of a more exalted order, made out of the zeal and devotion which characterized his study of the Torah and his prayer" (Zohar II, 210b).

The robes, or celestial garments worn by the righteous in *Gan Eden* reflect the quality of an individual's spiritual attainment: ". . . a man's good deeds done in this world draw from the celestial resplendency of light a garment with which he may be invested when he comes to appear before the Holy Blessed One. Appareled in that raiment, he is in a state of bliss and feasts his eyes on the radiant effulgence" (Zohar II, 229b).

Gan Eden is not static. The soul continues its post-mortem ascent and eventually enters Upper *Gan Eden*, "a compartment reserved for the pious of a higher grade" (Zohar II, 130a). Here the soul immerses in the celestial River of Light, *nehar dinur*, continuing the healing, purging remaining defilements (Zohar II, 211b).

In these supernal realms of Upper *Gan Eden* there are continual gradations, increasingly elevated abodes where the finely purified and righteous dwell, each soul in accordance with the accumulated merit of their life. The more spiritually developed a soul, the higher the realm in which it abides; "as the works of the righteous differ in this world, so do their place and lights differ in the next world (Zohar I,129a).

The *Gan Eden* phase of afterlife experience corresponds with the ritual act of observing a *Yahrzeit*, the anniversary of a death. According to Kabbalistic teachings, the act of recitation of a *Kaddish* at the time of a *Yahrzeit* elevates the soul every year to a higher sphere in *Gan Eden*. In remembering the deceased, the living have the ability to assist a disembodied soul sojourn through *Gan Eden*.

Tzror Ha-Hayyim
Return to the Source

According to Kabbalistic tradition, the soul's repose in *Gan Eden* is not eternal. Medieval Kabbalah delineates one additional realm of the afterlife journey. After completing a stay *Gan Eden*, souls enter *Tzror Ha-Hayyim*, "the bond of life," "source of life," or literally, "the bundle of the living." *Tzror Ha-Hayyim* is said to be a cosmic storehouse of souls, the point of origination and termination for all souls in the universe. This endpoint of the journey is achieved by the most supernal elements of soul capable of direct perception of God: "The virtuous who are thought to be worthy to be bound up in *Tzror Ha-Hayyim* are privileged to see the glory of the supernal Holy King, and their abode is higher than that of all the holy angels" (Zohar III, 182b). *Tzror Ha-Hayyim* is an experience of spiritual union with the divine. However, according to Kabbalistic tradition, in certain cases, souls require further life adventures, and are forced to undergo *gilgul*, reincarnation, or re-embodiment.

Reincarnation and Resurrection

Two other motifs inherent to medieval mystical afterlife teachings are reincarnation, *gilgul,* and resurrection of the dead, *tehiyat ha-metim.*

Medieval Kabbalah infused an entirely new afterlife concept into Jewish tradition— the doctrine of *gilgul,* transmigration or reincarnation. The Kabbalists taught that after sojourning through the post-mortem realms, many souls are eventually reborn, and through physical re-embodiment bring about further restitution for wrong-doings of a previous life.

The doctrine of *gilgul* first appeared in *Sefer Bahir,* ca. 1150-1200, as an esoteric doctrine explicated indirectly through metaphor and parable. Over the next century, *gilgul* became a more widespread belief, and from the Zohar onwards, the notion of reincarnation of the soul became normative in Kabbalistic circles. Within Zohar are explicit discourses on reincarnation teaching that "all souls, must undergo transmigration; but men do not perceive the ways of the Holy One . . . they perceive not the many transmigrations . . . which the Holy One accomplishes" (Zohar III, 99b).

For the early Kabbalists, *gilgul* offered those guilty of sexual transgressions opportunity to experience further restitution. Through rebirth, one was given the gift of another lifetime to make amends for sins committed.

In harmonizing teachings on *gilgul* with Rabbinic theology, Zohar asserted that the extent of one's obedience to the *mitzvot* determined whether or not one had to undergo *gilgul*. Ultimately, the aim of *gilgul* was to further purify the soul and provide more opportunities for self improvement and the fulfilling of *mitzvot*.

Fully committed to Rabbinic tradition, the Kabbalists embraced the doctrine of *tehiyat ha-metim*, physical resurrection of the dead at the end-of-days. However, for the Kabbalists, the resurrected physical body would be totally spiritualized and transformed. The belief put forth was that following judgment at the end-of-days, the radiant perfected soul would re-enter a fully resurrected body.

Over time, the Kabbalistic communities, particularly in the town of Safed in Palestine, downplayed the need for bodily resurrection. Belief in physical resurrection could not be harmonized with the spiritual, metaphysical cosmology of Lurianic Kabbalah. Resurrection was interpreted in a spiritual sense as a materialization of the spiritual body. Over time, it was taught that souls which had not fully evolved a spiritual body, at the time of collective resurrection would materialize on earth in order to fulfill any remaining *mitzvot*.

Ultimately, for the Kabbalists, resurrection itself is not the ultimate state of being. The fully awakened soul within a spiritualized, resurrected body was seen as divinity itself fully realized. The ultimate attainment was union with the Divine Being, the soul absorbed in the Godhead itself.

The rich heritage of Kabbalistic afterlife teachings were incorporated into Hasidism, and infused into Eastern European folk culture. However, with modernity and the advent of the Enlightenment, medieval mystical teachings on the afterlife were rejected or ignored. Today, there is a thriving curiosity about Jewish views around the afterlife, and once again the legacy of mystical afterlife teachings is being revived and explored.[22]

Deathbed Stories of the Hasidic Masters

The Baal Shem Tov's Death

When the Baal Shem Tov fell ill shortly before his death, he would not take to his bed. His body grew weak, his voice faint, and he would sit alone in his room meditating. On the eve of Shavuot, the last evening of his life, his disciples gathered around him and he spoke to them about the giving of the Torah at Mount Sinai. In the morning, he requested that all of them gather together in his room, and he gave his final instructions for burial to members of the *Hevra Kaddisha*. Afterwards he asked for a *siddur* (prayer book) and said: "I wish to spend some time communing with *Hashem Yitbarakh* (the Name, may He be blessed).

Then, after his time spent in prayer and preparation for greeting the Angel of Death, he told his disciples that as a sign, at the moment of his death, the two clocks in the house would stop. The Baal Shem Tov then asked his disciples to sing Reb Michal Zlotchover's melody, and they did so . . . After a while, the Baal Shem Tov began to describe how the soul was leaving his body, first through the extremities, slowly, slowly . . . slowly . . . Then in a quiet voice, he said: "Now I can no longer speak with you." His disciples looked and noticed that at the moment, one clock in the house had stopped.

The Baal Shem Tov then motioned for his disciples to cover him with blankets and he began to shake and tremble as he did when praying the silent prayer. Then, finally, he grew quiet, inhaled his last breath of air, and there was no exhalation, only stillness, peace. At that moment, the disciples noticed that the second clock in the house had stopped too. And those who buried the Baal Shem Tov said they had seen his soul ascend towards the heavens as a blue flame.[23]

The Death of Reb Shlomo of Karlin

When Reb Shlomo of Karlin was living in Ludmir, the Russians put down a revolt of the Poles in that region. The Russian commander who had entered the town, gave his men permission to loot at will for two hours. It was the Sabbath, and the Jews were gathered in the House of Prayer. Reb Shlomo was praying in such ecstasy that he heard nothing and saw nothing that went on around him. Just then, a tall cossack came limping along, went up to the window, looked in, and pointed his gun. In a ringing voice, the rabbi was saying the words, "For thine, O Lord, is the kingdom," when his little grandson, who was standing beside him, timidly tugged at his coat, and he awoke from ecstasy. But the bullet had already struck him in the side. "Why did you fetch me down?" he asked. When they brought him to his house, he had them open the Zohar (the Book of Splendor) at a certain passage and prop it up in front of him while they bound his wound. It stayed there, open before his eyes until the following Wednesday, when he died.[24]

The Death of Reb Michal of Zlotchov

In the last two years before his death, Rabbi Michal fell into a trance of ecstasy time after time. On these occasions, his face would glow and one could see that he clung to the higher life, rather than earthly existence. His children were always careful to rouse him from his ecstasy at the right moment, as they feared his soul had only one small step to pass over from this world. Once, after the third Sabbath meal, he went to the House of Study as usual and sang songs of praise. He returned home, entered his room unaccompanied, and began to pace the floor. His daughter, who was passing his door, heard him repeat over and over: "Willingly did Moses die! Willingly did Moses die!" She was greatly troubled and called one of her brothers. When he entered he found his father lying on the floor on his back, and heard him whisper the last word of the confession, "One,"s with his last breath.[25]

Psalms of Healing

Have mercy on me Lord, for I languish;
heal me, O Lord, for my bones shake
with terror.
Psalm 6: 3

O Lord, my God, I cried to You, and
You healed me.
Psalm 30: 2

The troubles of my heart are enlarged;
O bring me out of my distresses! Look
upon my affliction and my pain;
and forgive my sins.
Psalm 25: 17-18

Let me hear joy and gladness, that the
bones which you have broken may
rejoice.
Create in me a clean heart, O God; and
renew a constant spirit inside me.
Psalm 51: 10, 12

Hear my prayer, O Lord, and let my cry
reach you.
Do not hide your face from me in the
day when I am in trouble;
incline your ear to me; answer me
speedily in the day when I call.

    Psalm 102: 2-3

Crossing the Bar

Sunset and evening star,
And one clear call for me!
And may there be no moaning of the bar,
When I put out to sea,

But such a tide as moving seems asleep,
Too full for sound and foam,
When that which drew from out the
  boundless deep
Turns again home.

Twilight and evening bell,
And after that the dark!
And may there be no sadness of farewell,
When I embark;

For tho' from out our bourne of Time
  and Place
The flood may bear me far,
I hope to see my Pilot face to face
When I have crost the bar.[26]

— Alfred, Lord Tennyson

For Further Reading

Address, Richard. ed. *A Time to Prepare: A Practical Guide for Individuals and Families in Determining A Jewish Approach to Making Personal Arrangements, Establishing Medical Care and Embracing Rituals at the End of Life.* New York: UAHC Press, 2002.

Baron, Joel and Sara Paasche-Orlow. *Deathbed Wisdom of the Hasidic Masters: The Book of Departure and Caring for People at the End of Life.* Woodstock, VT: Jewish Lights, 2016.

Brener, Anne. *Mourning and Mitzvah: A Guided Journal for Walking the Mourner's Path Through Grief to Healing.* 2nd Edition. Woodstock, VT: Jewish Lights, 2013.

Brenner, Daniel S., et al. *Embracing Life & Facing Death: A Jewish Guide to Palliative Care.* New York: National Center for Learning and Leadership, 2002.

Diamant, Anita. *Saying Kaddish: How to Comfort the Dying, Bury the Dead and Mourn As A Jew.* New York: Schocken Books, 1998.

Ellison, Kosher Paley and Matt Weingast. eds. *Awake at the Bedside: Contemplative Teachings on Palliative and End-of-Life Care.* Somerville, MA: Wisdom

Publications, 2016.

Freeman, David L. and Judith Z. Abrams. *Illness and Health in the Jewish Tradition Writings from the Bible to Today*. Philadelphia, PA: Jewish Publication Society, 1999.

Halkin, Hillel. *After One-Hundred and-Twenty: Reflecting on Death, Mourning, and the Afterlife in the Jewish Tradition*. Princeton, NJ: Princeton University Press, 2016.

Hurwitz, Peter Joel, et al. *Jewish Ethics and the Care of End-of-Life Patients: A Collection of Rabbinical, Bioethical, Philosophical and Juristic Opinions*. Jersey City, NJ: Ktav Publishing House, 2006.

Raphael, Simcha Paull. *Afterlife and the Grief Journey: Jewish Pastoral Care for the Bereavement*. Boulder, CO: Albion-Andalus Books, 2015.

Raphael, Simcha Paull. *Jewish Views of the Afterlife*. Revised second edition. Lanham, MD: Rowman & Littlefield, 2009.

Raphael, Simcha Paull. *Living and Dying in Ancient Times: Death, Burial and Mourning in Biblical Tradition*. Boulder, CO: Albion-Andalus Books, 2015.

Singh, Kathleen Dowling. *The Grace in Dying*. San Francisco: Harper San Francisco, 1998.

NOTES AND REFERENCES

1. This story is found in: Stephen Levine, *Who Dies? An Investigation of Conscious Living and Conscious Dying* (Garden City, NY: Anchor Books, 1982), p. 272.

2. See Stanislav Grof, *Books of the Dead: Manuals for Living and Dying* (New York: Thames and Hudson, 1994), pp. 7-26, Grof, *The Ultimate Journey: Consciousness and the Mystery of Death* (Ben Lomand, CA: MultiDisciplinary Association for Psychedelic Studies, 2006), pp. 77-118.

3. Avriel Bar-Levav, "Leon Modena and the Invention of the Jewish Death Tradition" in *Aryeh Yishag: Rabbi Yehudah Aryeh Modenah ve-olamo*, edited by David Joshua Malkiel (Jerusalem: Hebrew University Magnes Press, 2003), pp. 85-102.

4. David Sclar, "The History and Development of the Taharah Ritual." Paper presented to the Chevra Kaddisha and Jewish Cemetery Conference, Atlanta, GA (June 8, 2010).

5. See Sylvie-Anne Goldberg, *Crossing the Jabbok: Illness and Death in Ashkenazi Judaism in Sixteenth through Nineteenth Century Prague*, trans. Carol Cossman (Berkeley: University of California Press, 1996).

6. Perry Raphael Bank (ed.), *The Rabbinical Assembly Rabbi's Manual, Vol. I* (New York: The Rabbinical Assembly, 1998), pp. D-23-D-26; Reuven Bulka (ed.) - *The RCA Lifecycle Madrikh* (New York: Rabbinical Council of American, 1995), pp. 129-137; Donald Goor, (ed.), *For Sacred Moments: The CCAR Life-Cycle Guide: Mourning*, (New York: Central Conference of American Rabbis, 1988), pp. 3-9.

7. A few notable exceptions are Shafir Lobb (ed.), *To Life! Bedside Prayers: Specially Compiled for Care facilities such as Hospitals, Nursing Homes, and Similar Facilities* (Rabbi Shafir Lobb, 2011), a self-published collection of original poems and prayers; Rabbi Simkha Y. Weintraub (ed.), *Healing of Soul, Healing of Body: Spiritual Leaders Unfold the Strength and Solace in Psalms* (Woodstock, VT: Jewish Lights Publishing, 1994), an exploration of ten Psalms for healing; and Alden Solovy, *Jewish Prayers of Hope and Healing* (USA: Kavanot Press, 2013), a wonderful, self-published collection of various prayers for grief, loss, illness and healing. None of these books can be seen specifically as a "deathbed manual" per se.

8. Zalman Schachter-Shalomi, *The Gates of Prayer: Twelve Talks on Davvenology* (Boulder, CO: Albion-Andalus Books, 2011), p. 31.

9. Larry Dossey, *Healing Words: The Power of Prayer and the Practice of Medicine* (New York: HarperCollins Publishers, 1994).

10. Cecily Saunders, et. al. (eds.), *Hospice: The Living Idea* (London: Edward Arnold, 1981).

11. Schachter-Shalomi, pp. 1-2.

12. Abraham Joshua Heschel, "Prayer" in *Moral Grandeur and Spiritual Audacity*, edited by Susannah Heschel (New York: Farrar, Strauss and Giroux, 1996), p. 341.

13. English translation, Ron Aigen (ed.), *Hadesh Yameinu: Renew Our Days: A Book of Jewish Prayer and Meditation* (Montreal, QC: Congregation Dorshei Emet, 1996), pp. 35-36.

14. Adapted from Goor, Section 2.1, p. 11.

15. Aigen, p. 130.

16. Rami Shapiro, *Last Breaths: A Guide to Easing Another's Dying* (Miami: Temple Beth Or, 1993), pp. 21-22.

17. Bank, pp. D-25-D-26.

18. Hyman E. Goldin (ed.), *HaMadrikh: The Rabbi's Guide* (New York: Hebrew Publishing Co., 1956), pp. 108-109.

19. See Robert F. Thurman, *The Tibetan Book of the Dead: Liberation Through Understanding In The Between* (New York: Bantam Books, 1994).

20. With thanks to Rabbi Nadya Gross.

21. With thanks to Rabbi Tsurah August, Jewish Hospice Network, Philadelphia, PA.

22. Adapted from Simcha Paull Raphael, *Jewish Views of the Afterlife* Revised 2nd edition, (Lanham, MD: Rowman and LittleField, Publishers), 2009; and Simcha Paull Raphael, "Afterlife: Medieval Judaism" in *Encyclopedia of Bible and Its Reception*, Vol. 1. (Berlin: Vaerlag Walter de Gruyter, 2009).

23. Martin Buber, *Tales of the Hasidim: Vol. I: Early Masters* (New York: Schocken Books, 1977), pp. 83-84.

24. *Ibid*, p. 284.

25. *Ibid*, p. 286.

26. Karen Hodder (ed.), *The Works of Alfred, Lord Tennyson* (London: Wordsworth Editions, Ltd., 1994) p. i.

May the Angels Carry You: Jewish Songs of Comfort for Death, Dying and Mourning

Rabbi Geela Rayzel Raphael

THIS COLLECTION OF SONGS and prayers is based upon the cycle of traditional Jewish liturgical moments dealing with death and loss.

Heartfelt and contemplative, these various songs were recorded in response to real life events of grief and transition. Several selections are designed to support the needs of the dying and their loved ones, chants and prayers for the deathbed. Other songs can be used to console and support grieving family and friends and to provide *nihum avelim*, comfort for the bereaved. These songs can also be incorporated into funeral and *shiva* rituals.

This collection of contemporary liturgical songs expands the repertoire for cantors, rabbis, members of the *hevra kaddisha*, chaplains, caregivers and others involved in this holy work.

For information on album purchase and lyrics see www. shechinah.com

דעת DA'AT INSTITUTE
DEATH AWARENESS, ADVOCACY *and* TRAINING

THE DA'AT INSTITUTE is dedicated to providing death awareness education and professional development training. Working in consultation with synagogues, churches, hospice programs and other types of community organizations, THE DA'AT INSTITUTE offers:

1. *Educational Programs* on death, dying, bereavement, and the spirituality of end-of-life issues and concerns.

2. *Professional Development Training* to clergy, health care and mental health professionals and educators working with the dying and bereaved.

3. *Bereavement and Hospice Counseling Services* to individuals and families through counseling, professional referral and bereavement support groups.

4. *Rituals of Transition* for dying, burial, bereavement, unveiling and memorialization, helping families create meaningful rituals of passage.

5. *Printed and Audio-Visual Resources* on the various facets of dealing with grief and loss, and on the spirituality of death and afterlife.

The DA'AT INSTITUTE
1211 Ansley Avenue
Melrose Park, PA 19027
drsimcha@daatinstitute.net
www.daatinstitute.net

Reb Simcha Paull Raphael, Ph.D. is Founding Director of the Da'at Institute for Death Awareness, Advocacy and Training (www.daatinstitute.net). He received his doctorate in Psychology from the California Institute of Integral Studies and was ordained as a Rabbinic Pastor by Rabbi Zalman Schachter-Shalomi. He is Associate Faculty in the Psychology Department of Bryn Athyn College, Adjunct Faculty in Graduate Religion at LaSalle University, and works as a psychotherapist and spiritual director in Philadelphia. A Fellow of the Rabbis Without Borders Network, he has written extensively on death and afterlife and is author of the groundbreaking, *Jewish Views of the Afterlife*.

36760335R00077

Made in the USA
Middletown, DE
10 November 2016